Foundations of Our Faith

David Laton

ISBN: 978-0-89098-888-6

Nashville, TN 37215

Cover design by Jonathan Edelhuber

ACKNOWLEDGEMENTS

I appreciate the inspiration and encouragement from my fellow Christians as I have had so many wonderful opportunities to grow in the grace and knowledge of our Lord and Savior. I specifically offer thanks to my friends Guy and Vicki Wood as I have seen their deep love for the deaf and hard of hearing. I've marveled many times with tears in my eyes as I've seen the poetry and dance of Vicki's hands as she shares God's Word to that community.

I also thank my friend Robert Vickrey as he continues the work Vicki started. I've come to regard Robert as a true friend and colleague.

And, I thank my friend, mentor, and shepherd Dr. Jerry Cantrell as he continues to encourage me, teach me, and demonstrate God's grace every day.

One more, please bear with me, special thanks goes out to my dear friend and sister in Christ, Ruth McMurphy Lee. I appreciate her diligence in proofreading and editing my work. As we say in Alabama, "Bless her heart!"

TABLE OF CONTENTS

INTRODUCTION

This book is designed to supplement classroom or small group instruction. Effort should be made by students to work through the material before coming to class so they come as "educated learners." In this way their questions may be answered and deeper levels of learning achieved. The better prepared students are the more they will be able to participate and learn, and most importantly, to understand God's will for their lives.

Encourage students to keep their Bibles open as they work through these lessons so they may see and learn God's Word from the source. It is through God's Word that we learn His will and grow to become who He wants us to become, Christ-like.

Also note at the beginning of each lesson the objective for the lesson and theme verse. This is provided to help students organize their thoughts and to determine if they are achieving the goals of the study.

LESSON 1

INTRODUCTION TO THE BIBLE

OBJECTIVE

The objective of this lesson is for students to identify (1) what the Bible is; (2) why the Bible is important; (3) and how the Bible is organized.

KEY VERSE

"All Scripture is breathed out by God and profitable for teaching, for reproof, for correction, and for training in righteousness, that the man of God may be complete, equipped for every good work."
2 Timothy 3:16-17

KEY LESSON POINTS

The Bible is God's Word.

Jesus is the center of the Bible story.

The Bible shows how we are saved.

What the Bible Is

The Bible is the Word of God. There are many Scriptures stating this or implying this. Perhaps the most common is the theme text for this lesson, 2 Timothy 3:16-17. The Bible was written by approximately 40 different men living in several different countries and different time periods. It was written between 1400 B.C. and A.D. 90. The Bible was written in three languages: Hebrew, Aramaic, and Greek. Today we have several translations in many different languages, but all are based on the three original biblical languages.

Despite these differences, God inspired, or moved, the writers to keep focused on a primary message: man's redemption through one central figure—Jesus, the Son of God.

Why the Bible Is Important

The Bible is a book God uses to show us what He is like, who He is, and what He likes and dislikes. So it is through God's Word that He speaks to us today. It is important to our eternal salvation that we understand and obey the Bible. We will explore in later lessons what specifically those things are. But be comforted in knowing that we serve a loving God who wants to show us His will and His love.

How the Bible Is Organized

The Bible is divided into two primary parts: the Old Testament and the New Testament. Both have a purpose in and of themselves but also focus on Jesus as the central purpose. The Old Testament points to Jesus as the savior of mankind. The New Testament gives us the history and teachings of Jesus on earth, the start of the church, and how the church spread to all the world.

ACTIVITY

The Bible is the ________________ of ________________.

In your own words, state why you think the Bible is important.

____

____

____

____

____

____

The Bible was written by _______ different men between _____ B.C. through A.D. _______.

What are the three original languages in which the Bible was written?

____

____

____

The Old Testament points to ______________ as the savior of mankind.

The New Testament gives us the:

____

____

____

The Pentateuch

The Old Testament

The Old Testament has 39 books divided into five sections, each with a specific purpose. It is also known as "The Old Law."

The first five books of the Old Testament were written by Moses around 1400 B.C. They are referred to the "Five Books of Moses" or the "Pentateuch." You may also hear them referred to as the "Torah." It is in this part we learn how God created man, man's sin, and how God began to put His plan in place to save man. In this part we also learn how God gave Moses the Ten Commandments and how to live according to His will.

ACTIVITY

The first five books of the Bible were written by __________ and are called the ____________________.

List the books of the Pentateuch in the order you find them in your Bible.

1. ____________________ The book of beginnings where we read of creation, man's fall, and how man will be saved.

2. ____________________ God delivers His people from Egyptian slavery and establishes His people as a nation.

3. ____________________ God gives rules to His people that show atonement for their sins, how to live holy lives, and rules for worship and sacrifice.

4. ____________________ The story of God's people wandering in the wilderness for 40 years because of their disobedience and lack of faith.

5. ____________________ Moses' great teaching to prepare Israel to finally enter the land promised to the people by God.

The Books of History

The next part of the Old Testament is known as the books of history. There are twelve books, which cover a large part of the history of Israel. They also contain some of the most important information of the entire story of the Bible. They tell of how Israel was formed and how it rose to power in the ancient world. It also tells of how Israel was punished by God for turning from God and to sin in many forms. But it also tells of God's faithfulness in restoring Israel. Many of the famous characters of the Bible such as David, Elijah, Solomon, Esther, and others are found in this section. Even people unfamiliar with the details of the Old Testament know many of these stories.

ACTIVITY

What is the purpose of the Books of History? They tell how Israel ____

____

____

____

List some famous Bible characters with whom you are familiar who are found in the Books of History. Which is your favorite?

____

____

____

____

List the 12 Books of History in the order you find them in your Bible.

1. ____________________	7. ____________________
2. ____________________	8. ____________________
3. ____________________	9. ____________________
4. ____________________	10. ____________________
5. ____________________	11. ____________________
6. ____________________	12. ____________________

The Books of Poetry

The next five books of the Old Testament are called the Books of Poetry. These are not the only "poetical" writings in the Bible but are classified as such as a group. These books of poetry describe the relationship man has with God and how God deals with man.

ACTIVITY

List the five books of poetry in the order in which they are listed in your Bible.

1. ______________________ Describes the suffering and trust of a man who loved God in spite of severe suffering and testing.

2. ______________________ Contains songs of praise and instruction.

3. ______________________ Shows God's practical wisdom for daily life.

4. ______________________ Teaches us the emptiness of a life without God, no matter how good it might seem to be.

5. ______________________ Celebrates the joy of God's plan for marriage between a man and woman.

The Prophets

Early in man's existence God spoke directly to the leaders of families. These were called the patriarchs. But then God began to speak to man through his prophets. A prophet was someone God used to communicate His message to the world. There were many prophets used by God other than those that wrote books of the Bible. The books named for the prophets in the Old Testament can be divided into two types: Major Prophets and Minor Prophets. The difference was the length of their writing, not their message. The Major Prophets wrote long books on what God gave them to say. The Minor Prophets wrote shorter books, but their messages were just as important.

The prophets came from a variety of backgrounds and spoke to different groups, often for different reasons. Sometimes they spoke to individuals as well as groups. Most of their message was to Israel, but sometimes it involved other nations God was using for His purposes.

The **Major** Prophets wrote their books approximately 750 and 550 B.C. The **Minor** Prophets wrote their books approximately between 840 and 400 BC.

ACTIVITY

How did God speak to man in the earliest days?

____

For what did God use prophets in the Old Testament?

____

What is the difference between the two types of prophets in the Old Testament?

____

____

____

List the Major Prophets in the order you find them in your Bible.

1. ____________________
2. ____________________
3. ____________________
4. ____________________
5. ____________________

List the Minor Prophets in the order you find them in your Bible.

1. ____________________
2. ____________________
3. ____________________
4. ____________________
5. ____________________
6. ____________________
7. ____________________
8. ____________________
9. ____________________
10. ____________________
11. ____________________
12. ____________________

The New Testament

There was a period of approximately 400 years between the last book of the Old Testament and the events we find in the life of Jesus. This period was a time of war with different nations ruling over Israel. It was also a time when we have no recorded direct communication from God to man.

All of this brought about a time when God decided it was right for Jesus to come to complete the plan He had put in place in Genesis 3:15 when God cursed Satan. The Apostle Paul wrote in Galatians 4:4-5,

> *"But when the fullness of time had come, God sent forth his Son, born of woman, born under the law, to redeem those who were under the law, so that we might receive adoption as sons."*

So now, in God's time (fullness of time), the world was ready for Jesus to come to earth. That is where the New Testament starts.

The New Testament, or New Covenant (promise), reveals Jesus Christ, the Redeemer of man. In it we find three parts, each with a specific purpose.

- The life of Jesus (The Gospels)
- The beginning of the Church and the spread of Christianity (Acts)
- Instructions for Christian Living (The Epistles, including Revelation)

ACTIVITY

How many years, approximately were between the last of the Old Testament books and the gospels? ____________________

Read Galatians 4:4-5. What does it say about when it was time for Jesus to come to earth?

____

____

Where does the New Testament start?

____

____

____

The Gospels

The detail of the life of Jesus is found in the first four books of the New Testament. These are also referred to as the "Gospels." The word *gospel* means good news. So these books are the good news of Jesus' coming to save mankind from sin. Basically, *salvation* means to reconcile man back to God. To *reconcile* something means to bring it back into balance. Salvation means that Jesus gave His life so that those who believe and obey His commands will be saved from their sins. Our lives and God would be back in balance. In a later lesson, we will study more about salvation and how we are saved.

Each Gospel was written to different people and emphasized different things. The Gospels do not conflict with one another. They bring out different views of events and teachings of Jesus. Some of the Gospels give more detail about the events, while others might not even mention that same event. Although the order of events might differ slightly among the gospels, the teachings are consistent.

ACTIVITY

Where do we find details of the life of Jesus?

___

What does the word *gospel* mean?

___

Who is the key figure in all four of the Gospels?

___

The Gospels

The Book of Matthew was written by the Apostle Matthew. An apostle is someone who speaks on behalf of the one he follows. Jesus selected 12 men, including Matthew, to be His apostles who would later teach all the world about Jesus.

We know Matthew was a tax collector. He was a Jew who wrote to Jews, about Jesus, who was a fellow Jew. The book of Matthew was specifically written to show that Jesus was the Jew's long-awaited Messiah. *Messiah* means promised deliverer, or savior. The people were looking for a savior to take them back to the days of glory found in the old times when Israel was a powerful nation feared and respected by the world. This was a misunderstanding of the nature of the promised Messiah and the purpose and teachings of Jesus. Jesus came to establish an eternal, spiritual kingdom, not a physical kingdom that passes away.

The Book of Mark was written by a disciple named Mark, sometimes called John Mark. *Disciple* means one who is a student or follower, so a disciple of Jesus is one who studies and follows His teachings.

Although not one of the original 12 apostles, Mark was a faithful follower of Jesus and a close friend of Peter. He wrote the Gospel of Mark as Peter told him the events that Peter witnessed as an apostle. Mark's intended audience were Romans who were the leading power of the day, ruling much of the civilized world. He emphasized the faithful, obedient service and sacrifice of Jesus.

The Book of Luke was written by a historian Luke. He also was not an apostle but faithful disciple of Jesus and a friend of Paul. Luke was careful to write down the history of Jesus' life as told by eyewitnesses. This would have included the apostles as well as others who traveled and learned from Jesus. Luke was not Jewish, so he was referred to as a Gentile or Greek. The words *gentile* and *Greek* are used in the Bible to refer to anyone not a Jew. So Luke's Gospel was written by a non-Jew to other non-Jews to tell the story of a Jewish man, Jesus. Luke emphasizes the historical facts of Jesus and shows the humanity of Jesus.

The Book of John was the last of the four Gospels. John was not only an apostle, but he was also a close friend of Jesus. John was with Jesus at important events such as his arrest, trial, and crucifixion. But he was also present at times when Jesus needed a close companion such as the time in the Garden of Gethsemane when Jesus was preparing to be arrested. John wrote his gospel to appeal to everyone teaching that Jesus was the Son of God.

ACTIVITY

________________ Written especially to Jews revealing Jesus Christ as their long-awaited Messiah.

________________ Written primarily to Roman citizens and shows Jesus as a faithful and obedient servant and sacrifice.

________________ Written to a gentile world and emphasizes the historical accuracy of the life of Jesus as well as the humanity of Jesus.

________________ Written to mankind in general showing Jesus as the true Son of God.

Acts ~ The Beginning of the Church

The beginning and growth of Christianity is recorded in the **Book of Acts.** Acts was written by Luke, the same author of the Gospel of Luke. The book was intended as a second volume and was addressed to a man named, Theophilus. It is thought that Theophilus was a Roman official that Luke had taught about Jesus.

Acts is divided into two major parts and has two main characters, Peter and Paul. The first part is from chapters 1 to 12. These tell the beginning of the church and the role Peter played in it. It includes many teachings by Peter and the other apostles.

The second part of Acts begins in Chapter 13 and goes through to the end of the book in Chapter 28. During this period, we see Paul and his role in spreading the gospel to the world.

ACTIVITY

Who are the two main characters in the book of Acts?

____

____

What are the two major parts of the book of Acts?

Acts 1 – 12 ____________________________

Acts 13 – 28 ____________________________

The Beginning of the Church

Acts begins with the period of time when Jesus was preparing to return to heaven. In the first chapter, He gives the apostles final instructions and then returns to heaven. Following this event, the apostles return to Jerusalem and wait for the promise Jesus had made. The apostles didn't know what to expect. They thought Jesus would return soon, so they continued in prayer. During this time, they selected a man named Matthias to replace Judas (you'll find out why he had to be replaced in another chapter) so that they had 12 men to be apostles, just as Jesus had done originally.

As the apostles were waiting, a great event happened. We call this the Day of Pentecost. On this day the apostles and others were gathered together, and the Holy Spirit appeared over each of them looking like small flames of fire. The apostles began to speak in other languages as the Holy Spirit gave them the ability. This was so that everyone would understand what was being said in their own language. This event drew a large crowd. Peter then stood before the crowd and began to tell them what had happened and why. He told the crowd about Jesus and how they were guilty of having put Jesus, the Son of God, to death. As a result, the crowd cried out to Peter asking what they had to do to be forgiven. Peter responded by telling them to repent and be baptized to gain forgiveness of their sins. That day more than 3,000 people obeyed what Peter told them to do.

Following the events of Pentecost, we begin to see the Church growing but remaining in Jerusalem. Acts goes on to tell how many, many other people came to learn about Jesus and obeyed the command given to repent and be baptized.

A period of much trouble followed for the Christians in the early church that included some being killed and punished in other ways. As a result, many of the early Christians were driven out of Jerusalem. Eventually they went into all the known world and taught about Jesus wherever they went.

ACTIVITY

The beginning of the Church is found in Acts 2.

What major event occurred in this chapter?

____

What did the people do who heard Peter's sermon?

____

Instructions for Christian Living – The Epistles

Acts shows us the beginning of the Church and how it was spread throughout the world. As you can imagine, as the early Christians began to return to their homes in many parts of the world, they faced many problems that would challenge their faith in God. As much as they could, the apostles tried to prepare them by teaching all that Jesus had taught them.

Many of these problems faced by the early Christians would be expected due to the difference of the Church and their role in it. But this would be even harder because of the persecution they would face from many who resisted the teachings of Jesus.

The early Christians did not have the New Testament as we have it today. In fact, they were in the process of writing it. It wasn't until sometime later that they would have had elders, church leaders, to help them. Unlike many of our elders today, they didn't have a lifetime of teaching and experience. They did have the apostles who would write letters to them about the problems and how to deal with them. They would also write to encourage and continue to teach them about Jesus.

These letters are also known as the Epistles. The word *epistle* means letter. Most of these letters were written by Paul, but others also wrote them, including Peter, James (the half-brother of Jesus), Jude (also a half-brother to Jesus), and John. We don't know for certain who wrote the book of Hebrews, but many believe it was Paul.

Instructions for Christian Living – The Epistles

Epistles written by Paul:

- Romans
- 1 & 2 Corinthians
- Galatians
- Ephesians
- Philippians
- Colossians
- 1 & 2 Thessalonians
- 1 & 2 Timothy
- Titus
- Philemon
- Hebrews (possibly)

General Epistles and Revelation:

- James
- 1 & 2 Peter
- 1, 2, 3 John
- Jude
- Revelation

Revelation is also a letter written by John to Christians throughout the area known as Asia (Revelation 1:4). It is considered by some to be a book of prophecy about the return of Jesus and the final judgment. It is often misunderstood and misused. The key to understanding Revelation is that Christians are to remain faithful, even under severe persecution. The book uses coded or symbolic language that shows that Christians would face persecution but that Jesus had already won the victory and would reward those who remained faithful, even unto death.

Many people try to use Revelation to predict the return of Jesus and judgment day. This is not a correct way to understand Revelation. We will study more about judgment in a later lesson.

Conclusion

One way we know that God loves us is that He wants us to know how to be saved from our sins and live as He would like for us to live. That is the main purpose of the Bible. We should try to learn as much as we can about God's Word and how to grow in our faith.

ACTIVITY

The epistles were ______________ written to early Christians to help them with problems they faced in their effort to remain faithful.

Who wrote most of the epistles?

____

What was the purpose of the book of Revelation?

____

____

____

In the spaces below, list the epistles in the order you find them in the Bible.

The epistles probably written by Paul.

1. ____________________ 8. ____________________
2. ____________________ 9. ____________________
3. ____________________ 10. ____________________
4. ____________________ 11. ____________________
5. ____________________ 12. ____________________
6. ____________________ 13. ____________________
7. ____________________ 14. ____________________

The general epistles and Revelation.

1. ____________________ 5. ____________________
2. ____________________ 6. ____________________
3. ____________________ 7. ____________________
4. ____________________ 8. ____________________

HOW THE BIBLE IS ORGANIZED

The Old Testament (39 Books)

PENTATEUCH	HISTORY	POETRY	PROPHECY	
			MAJOR PROPHETS	MINOR PROPHETS
Genesis	Joshua	Job	Isaiah	Hosea
Exodus	Judges	Psalms	Jeremiah	Joel
Leviticus	Ruth	Proverbs	Lamentations *	Amos
Numbers	I & II Samuel	Ecclesiastes	Ezekiel	Obadiah
Deuteronomy	I & II Kings	Song of Solomon	Daniel	Jonah
	I & II Chronicles			Micah
	Ezra			Nahum
	Nehemiah			Habakkuk
	Esther			Zephaniah
				Haggai
				Zechariah
				Malachi

Time Between The Testaments (Approximately 400 Years)

The New Testament (27 Books)

GOSPELS	HISTORY	LETTERS
Matthew	Acts	Romans
Mark		I & II Corinthians
Luke		Galatians
John		Ephesians
		Philippians
		Colossians
		I & II Thessalonians
		I & II Timothy
		Titus
		Philemon
		Hebrews **
		James
		I & II Peter
		I, II & III John
		Jude
		Revelation ***

God used 40 different men over approximately 1,500 years (1400 B.C. to A.D. 90) in writing the Bible.

* Lamentations was written by Jeremiah to express his grief over the destruction of Jerusalem.
** Although not known for certain, many consider Hebrews to have been written by Paul.
*** Some consider Revelation to be a "Book of Prophecy" in a section by itself.

LESSON 2

HOW TO STUDY THE BIBLE

OBJECTIVE

To learn how to study the Bible so that we may gain the full meaning of what God's Word tells us.

KEY VERSE

"Do your best to present yourself to God as one approved, a worker who has no need to be ashamed, rightly handling the word of truth."

2 Timothy 2:15

KEY LESSON POINTS

Understand the context.

Don't get distracted by minor details.

Understand how the parts of the Bible are related.

The first lesson was an overview of both the New Testament and the Old Testament, including how the Bible is organized and the major parts of both testaments. This chapter will focus on how to study the Bible. It is important to learn God's Word, but it is also important to put into action what you've learned.

Studying involves a purpose. Determine what you want to learn and why. Without a purpose, you won't learn as much about God's will as you should. Although it might be pleasant and there is certainly nothing wrong with just opening up God's Word and reading, you won't gain the most from that method. Think about how you read any other book. You usually don't start in the middle of a chapter and try to understand all that is in the book. So there should be an organized process for studying God's Word.

There are many reasons why people study the Bible. Some study the Bible to discover a way to solve a problem in their lives. Others might study to gain knowledge of who God is or to gain insights into life in general. Whatever the reason, you should know first why you are studying since this will guide your thoughts through the process.

Studying is both a physical and mental process. You should relax while you study. You need to have a place free from distractions. You should also try to have a set time and place for study. And you should have any items you need to help you study. For example, you might have something to write on so you can write your thoughts as you study. Sometimes while you study, the Holy Spirit gives you insight into what God's Word is telling you so you should consider writing it down for future reference.

ACTIVITY

Complete this statement: Studying involves a ______________.

Read 2 Timothy 2:15. In your own words, what is this verse telling you?

____

____

____

____

____

____

Studying the Bible

There are three general things to remember as you study God's Word.

1. Understand the context.

Context means we look at who wrote it, to whom it was written, why it was written, and how it relates to the words before and after. If you do not study the context, then you can easily misunderstand what is being said.

While reading a passage from God's Word, you should ask what question or problem is being addressed. You must look at how it was being answered by the writer or speaker. You must also look at how you can apply the truth of the passage to your life today.

Here's an example. Matthew 7:1 states,

"Judge not, that you be not judged."

People take this passage by itself and try to say that Jesus was not about judging people, so we also must not. If that is true, then they miss the point of what Jesus was saying and even worse, they miss the point of who and what Jesus was.

The point of that passage is that Jesus was teaching us that if we do judge, then we must be aware that we also will be judged by the same standard. He goes on to explain that we must make certain we are not overlooking our own sins.

2. Don't get distracted by minor details.

The Bible contains a lot of details about the lives of people of the time. Sometimes, these details are present to help you gain insights into what is happening, but they are not the main point that is being taught. If you focus too much on details, then you miss the main point that God wants you to understand.

Here's are some examples:

What kind of fruit did Adam and Eve eat? (Genesis 3) That's not the point of the story. The point is that they disobeyed God and were separated from Him.

Was it a fish or a whale that swallowed Jonah? (Jonah 1:17) That's not the point of the story. The story is about how we should follow God's commands, even when we might not desire to do so.

When will the world end? That's not the point. The point is that Jesus will return (Acts 1:10-11) and that we should be ready for it.

We are told in Romans 12:2 that we must transform our minds. This means that we allow God's Word to change who we are as we learn it and apply it to our lives. We do that when we remain focused on what God's Word is telling us.

3. Understand how the parts of the Bible are related.

Some read a part of the Bible as if it stands entirely alone, separated from the rest of Scripture. This greatly increases the chance that someone will misunderstand what is being taught. This is more than reading it in context. You must understand that the Bible is a story that unfolded over almost 1,500 years. It is the story of:

- How God created man.
- How man sinned.
- How God brought about the salvation of mankind through the sacrifice of Jesus.
- How God created a kingdom here on earth.
- How we are to live as citizens in God's kingdom.
- How to be ready for Jesus' return.

Every passage of Scripture makes sense as part of this grand story. To remove a single element and try to make it stand on its own will cause you to miss the point of the whole story.

ACTIVITY

What does *context* mean? ______________________________

____

What does *transforming our minds* mean? ________________

____

In the space below list the six major parts of the story of God and mankind found in the Bible.

1. ____

   ____

2. ____

   ____

3. ____

   ____

4. ____

   ____

5. ____

   ____

6. ____

   ____

Conclusion

Studying the Bible is important if you are to know and understand what God wants you to do to be saved and how He wants us to live. Bible study is something we must never stop doing because our lives change, and we put into practice what God's Word tells us. God's Word doesn't change, but we do. That also is part of what Paul tells us in Romans 12:2 about transforming our minds. This is a lifelong process. It is a journey that leads us to becoming who God wants us to be, just like his Son, Jesus. That is what being a Christian is about.

LESSON 3

WHO WAS JESUS?

OBJECTIVE

The objective of this lesson is for students to learn that Jesus is the Son of God and our Savior.

KEY VERSE

"But when the fullness of time had come, God sent forth his Son, born of woman, born under the law, to redeem those who were under the law, so that we might receive adoption as sons."

Galatians 4:4-5

KEY LESSON POINTS

Jesus is the Son of God.

Jesus died for our sins.

Jesus rose from the dead.

As you continue studying the foundations of our faith, you must understand who Jesus is. Being a Christian is about living a life that is completely focused on Jesus. Jesus is described by the Apostle Paul as a cornerstone (Ephesians 2:20). A cornerstone is the main part of a foundation upon which an entire building is built. So Jesus, as our cornerstone, is the One in whom we put our faith. He is the One we trust for our salvation.

The name of Jesus is one of the most well-known names throughout the world. Even people who do not believe that Jesus is the Son of God recognize His name. Some today call Jesus a prophet along with many other prophets from the Bible and history. During His time on earth, some thought Jesus was John the Baptist raised from the dead or the prophet Elijah reborn, or other well-known spiritual people. But to those that follow Jesus and believe in the Bible, Jesus is the Son of God. And He is also the Savior of mankind promised by God in Genesis 3.

Jesus is also known as the Christ. The word *Christ* means the Messiah, or Savior. Sometimes He is referred to as Jesus, sometimes Christ, and sometimes Jesus Christ. All are acceptable names for the same person.

ACTIVITY

Read Matthew 16:13-16 and answer the following questions.

What do the apostles say when Jesus asked them who people said He was? ______________________________

____

What does the apostle Peter say when Jesus asked, "But who do you say that I am?" ______________________

____

Who Was Jesus?

Here is what we know about Jesus from history. Jesus was born in Bethlehem, a small town south of Jerusalem. The land at the time of His birth was under the control of the Roman government. He was raised by His mother, Mary, and His earthly father, Joseph. Because the evil King Herod wanted to kill Jesus, the family moved to Egypt. Later His parents moved back and settled in the town of Nazareth, where He grew up; so He is sometimes called "Jesus of Nazareth." His father, Joseph, was a carpenter. Jesus also worked as a carpenter as He was growing up (Mark 6:3).

When Jesus was about 30, He began to teach and to do miracles that proved He was who He claimed to be—the Son of God. This time period is called His "earthly ministry." At the beginning of His earthly ministry, He had lots of people following Him. These followers were called disciples. A disciple is a follower or student. From this large group of disciples, He chose 12 men to be His apostles. An apostle is a messenger and speaks on behalf of the one they follow.

ACTIVITY

Where was Jesus born? ______________________________

Who were His earthly parents? ______________________________

Where did Jesus grow up? ______________________________

Who Was Jesus?

Jesus taught many things that were different than what the people of that time had been taught. Because of His teachings, many people followed Him, but not everyone agreed with Him. He also performed many miracles to heal people, feed people, but most of all to show that He was who He claimed to be.

Some of the people who did not believe Jesus was who He said He was were leaders of the Jewish faith. These men were teachers and other officials called by different titles. Some were called Pharisees. Others were called Scribes. Still others were called Priests. Because of His popularity and success, these Jewish leaders became jealous and resented Jesus. They soon plotted with the Roman government to have Him killed. We don't know why, but one of Jesus' apostles, Judas, betrayed Him to the Jewish leaders. Jesus was then arrested, put on trial, and executed by hanging on a cross. This method of execution is called crucifixion.

But the death of Jesus was not the end of the story. Three days after He was buried, Jesus rose from the dead. And for the next 40 days, He was seen by many people, sometimes by individuals, sometimes by small groups, and sometimes by large groups. After that time He went to the Mount of Olives outside of Jerusalem with only His apostles and gave them His final instructions:

> *"All authority in heaven and on earth has been given to me. Go therefore and make disciples of all nations, baptizing them in the name of the Father and of the Son and of the Holy Spirit, teaching them to observe all that I have commanded you. And behold, I am with you always, to the end of the age"* (Matthew 28:18-20).

After giving them this final instruction, He rose into heaven. While the apostles were looking up to try to see Him, an angel appeared to them and told them that one day Jesus would come back just as they saw Him leaving.

ACTIVITY

You will need your Bible to complete this activity.
This activity is designed for you to see from the Bible who Jesus was and what He did for us as our Savior.

Read the following Bible verses, and answer the questions that follow.

Luke 2:9-12

Who is the angels saying will be the Savior?

____

What was the sign for them about the Savior?

____

John 1:29

Who is John talking about in this verse as the Lamb of God?

____

What did John say the Lamb of God would do?

____

Matthew 3:13 – 17

Why did John not want to baptize Jesus?

____

What was the importance of what happened immediately after Jesus was baptized?

John 10:10 – 11

What does Jesus promise us in regards to life?

What does Jesus say the good shepherd does for his sheep?

LESSON 4

WHAT IS SALVATION?

OBJECTIVE

The objective of this lesson is to understand what salvation is and our response to God's invitation.

KEY VERSE

"For God so loved the world, that he gave his only Son, that whoever believes in him should not perish but have eternal life."

John 3:16

KEY LESSON POINTS

Salvation comes from obeying the teachings of Jesus.

Salvation means to be right with God.

Hear, believe, repent, confess, and be baptized.

Up to this point, you have learned how the Bible is organized and who Jesus is. As you studied these lessons, you read about the word *salvation,* which means giving your life to God and obeying the teachings of Jesus. Salvation is found only through Christ Jesus (John 14:1-7).

There is more to this than just a simple statement of belief about Jesus and being baptized. In this lesson, you will look at what salvation is and how we are saved. Please have your Bible for this lesson because each part of what you are going to learn is found in the Bible. You must do what God says rather than what someone else says. Let's begin by learning more about what salvation is.

Salvation means to be in a relationship with God that frees you from the consequences of your sins. Sins separate us from God and must be removed before we can again be a part of God. If you do not become a part of God, then you are separated from Him now and after your death. On the other hand, if you accept the salvation that He offers, your sins are forgiven, and you are not separated from Him now or after your death.

ACTIVITY

Read the Scriptures listed below, and explain what you think the verse is saying.

Romans 3:23 ______________________________________

____

____

1 John 3:4 ______________________________________

____

____

1 John 1:8 ____________________________________

____

____

Romans 14:12 ________________________________

____

____

What separates you from God?

____

____

____

____

Salvation

None of us can be good enough by ourselves. God offers us this salvation even though there is nothing we can do to earn it or deserve it. We find that God loves us so much that He sent Christ to die in our place.

ACTIVITY

Read the Scriptures listed below, and explain what you think the verse is saying.

John 14:6 ____

____

____

____

Acts 4:11-12 ____

____

____

____

Romans 5:6 -11 ____

____

____

____

Examples of Salvation

When you studied about how the Bible was organized, you learned that the book of Acts was about how the Church as started and how it grew. In the book of Acts, you will read how people are saved and added to the Church. Acts includes many examples of what people were taught and what they did, and in these examples, we find God's will for our salvation. Let us look at some of these examples to find out what we also must do to be saved from our sins. Always remember though, we do not earn our salvation. It is granted to us by God's grace and our faith (Ephesians 2:8).

The First Gospel Sermon

Beginning with Acts 1, we find the apostles and other disciples gathered together. We read in Acts 2 that suddenly they heard a noise described as sounding like rushing wind. The disciples saw what seemed to be small flames over each apostle's head. This was God's Spirit, which gave them the understanding of Jesus' message and the ability to speak in the language of all the people of the city who had gathered there.

Following this event, the disciples began to teach about Jesus. The people were amazed that these men could speak in their own language. Peter began to explain to the people how this was happening and what Scripture said concerning whom Jesus was. Many believed what Peter and the disciples said and wanted to know what to do to be saved. Peter told them that they must repent of their sins and to be baptized in the name of the Father, Son, and the Holy Spirit. He then told them that they would receive forgiveness for their sins. The word Peter used was *remission*. It means to have a debt canceled or forgiven. So the people who did what Peter said had their debt of sin cancelled or forgiven. That day about 3,000 people did what Peter taught them. The Bible then says that they were added to the Church meaning they were saved.

Repent means to turn away or change the way they had been living. To be baptized "in the name of" means under the authority of or according to the will of. So this means that the people were to change their lives from how they had been living and to begin obeying God, Jesus, and the Holy Spirit. This obedience involved baptism. The baptism represents dying, being buried, and rising from the dead, just as Jesus did. It is also called a "new birth." This is to what Jesus was referring in John 3:3 when talking to a man named Nicodemus about eternal life.

> *"Jesus answered him, "Truly, truly, I say to you, unless one is born again he cannot see the kingdom of God."*

ACTIVITY

Where only do we find salvation?

___

Is there anything we can do to earn our salvation?

___

What does the word *remission* mean?

___

___

What does the word *repent* mean?

___

___

Read Acts 2:38. In your own words, what does Peter tell the people they must do to be saved?

___

___

___

Salvation

The Ethiopian Official

Many people enjoy reading of the conversion of the **Ethiopian official** in Acts 8:26-39. We read of an important civil official returning from worshiping in the temple in Jerusalem. The Lord told one of the disciples named Philip to go to the road that ran down from Jerusalem to Gaza. Philip obeyed and saw an Ethiopian official riding in a chariot studying God's Word from the Old Testament book of Isaiah. Philip was told by the Holy Spirit to approach him. Philip began speaking to the man by asking him if he understood what he was studying. The man answered that he needed someone to explain it to him. So Philip began from where the man was studying and taught him about Jesus.

As they went on, they came by some water. The man asked Philip why he shouldn't be baptized. Philip told him that if he believed what he had been taught about Jesus then he could. The man answered that he believed. So both Philip and the man went down into the water where Philip baptized him. Scripture goes on to say that the man then went on his way rejoicing.

Again, we see God's will for our salvation. The Ethiopian was studying God's Word. Philip taught him Jesus so we see the **hearing** of God's Word. We read where he **confessed**. And we read where he was immediately **baptized** as soon as they came to some water. It is important to note that Scripture teaches that he rejoiced ***after*** his baptism. We learn from this that the salvation was the reason for his rejoicing and that it occurred *after* he was baptized.

ACTIVITY

Why had the Ethiopian been to Jerusalem?

____

What was the Ethiopian doing when Philip saw him?

____

After they came across water and he ordered the chariot to stop, what did the Ethiopian and Philip do?

____

The Conversion of the Apostle Paul

In Acts 9:1-19 we learn about the events of the apostle Paul's salvation, a well-known example of salvation.

As Acts begins, this man was known as Saul. He was well-known man and quite knowledgeable of Jewish law and was strongly against anyone teaching about Jesus Christ. He had been given permission by the Jewish leaders to find Christians and put them in prison. He was on his way to a city called Damascus to do that when suddenly a bright light shown around him. The light blinded him, and he fell to the ground.

He heard a voice asking him why he was persecuting Him. Saul didn't know to whom he was talking. The voice replied that it was Jesus whom he was persecuting. Jesus then told him to go to Damascus where he would be told what to do. As Saul got up, he found he was still blind. Meanwhile in Damascus, a Christian named Ananias was told by Jesus to go to Saul and teach him what to do. As Ananias began to teach him, Saul regained his eyesight. Scripture tells us that Saul immediately got up and was baptized.

Again, we see God's will for us concerning salvation. Saul (Paul) **heard** God's Word from Ananias. He obviously **believed** because he obeyed. We don't have a clear wording that he **repented** except that we can see from his actions later and through the remainder of his life that he certainly changed from persecuting Christians to championing the gospel. The same applies for the process of **confessing**. Then we see Paul immediately being **baptized**, even before taking food to regain his strength. Note that Paul himself began to preach about Jesus immediately after his baptism.

ACTIVITY

Why was Paul going to Damascus?

___

Whose voice was talking to Paul while he lay on the ground?

___

What did the voice tell Paul to do?

___

What did Paul do after Ananias taught him?

___

The Philippian Jailer

Acts 16:23-14 tells the story of a man who worked as a jailer and how he and his family were saved.

The apostle Paul and a fellow Christian named Silas had been preaching in the city of Philippi when they were arrested, beaten, and thrown in prison. That night, even though they were chained up and suffering from the beating, the two men were singing and praising God. Suddenly, an earthquake set them free from their chains. The jailer in charge thought that the prisoners had escaped. He was just about to kill himself when Paul called out to him that they were all there. The jailer fell at Paul's feet and asked what he must do to be saved. Paul's reply was for him to believe on the Lord Jesus and he would be saved. The jailer took them to his house, cared for their wounds, and was immediately baptized. The Bible finishes this account by telling us that the jailer was filled with joy because he and his family had come to believe in Jesus.

In this account, we see the elements of salvation come together. The jailer **heard** Paul tell him to believe in Jesus. We see that he **believed**. He **repented** from being one who persecuted Christians to one caring for them. We don't clearly see a **confession**, but we see him acting on his belief so we can understand that he did. An important point to note here is that the Bible says he was **baptized** that night. This means that he recognized that all of what had happened was important but that he also needed to be baptized.

ACTIVITY

How did Paul and Silas respond when the jailer asked how to be saved?

____

List what the jailer did that led to his salvation.

____

How soon after Paul and Silas taught the jailer about salvation was he baptized?

____

The Roman Soldier

Let's look a final example of salvation from the early church. Of all the examples, the salvation of a Roman soldier named **Cornelius** is one with which many identify. This is the first person who was not a Jew to be saved. We read about this account as found in Acts 10:1-48.

Cornelius was a Roman soldier in Italy. He held the position of Centurion, which means he was in charge of 100 other soldiers. This gave him a great deal of influence and power in the Roman army and in the area where he served.

Cornelius was not an ordinary Roman soldier because he is described as a devout, God-fearing man. He gave to those in need and prayed regularly to God. God appreciated Cornelius and caused him to have a vision in which he was told to send for the apostle Peter. So Cornelius sent his servants to get him.

While this was happening to Cornelius, Peter was praying, and God caused him to have a vision in which he showed him some animals considered by Jewish law to be forbidden to eat. He told Peter to eat the animals. Peter refused, but God explained that he was not to call anything unclean. In other words, what God said was to be obeyed. While Peter was wondering what this vision meant, Cornelius's servants arrived. The Holy Spirit told Peter to go with them.

The next day Peter went with the men. When Peter arrived, he explained that God had told him to not call anything unclean and to go with the servants. Cornelius told Peter that he had been told by an angel to send for him.

Peter began to teach Cornelius and his household about Jesus and how He was for all men, not just the Jews. While Peter was speaking, the Holy Spirit appeared to Cornelius and those gathered there just as He had to the apostles on the day of Pentecost. The people experienced the same ability to speak in other languages. Peter immediately realized that this meant that the Gentiles, or non-Jews, were also to receive the opportunity for salvation. He then ordered that they be baptized in the name of Jesus.

From this event you should see that even though Cornelius was a religious man, he still was not saved. Why else would God have bothered to send Peter to teach him? He was taught by Peter about Jesus and then he and his household were baptized. Many of us today are believers in God but still need to learn the truth from Scripture about salvation that is only found in Jesus. We see that the gospel is for everyone, not a select group. Jesus is the Savior for humanity as well as our personal savior.

This event teaches us that many are living religious lives but are doing so in error. The question is, "Have they followed what Jesus said about salvation and demonstrated by the disciples and the early church?"

ACTIVITY

Who was Cornelius? ______________________________

What did Peter command after the Holy Spirit had come upon Cornelius and his household? ______________________________

____

Who must obey the gospel today? ______________________________

Conclusion

From our study of what Jesus taught and the examples of salvation found in the Book of Acts, we see God's will for us to follow today. Sometimes we see a clear picture of each element. Other times we must understand from the reading that it must have happened. What we do see is that in every case, they **heard** God's Word, responded to in some form showing they **believed**, and were **baptized**. From this we must examine ourselves and answer what we must do to be saved.

Through this lesson, you've seen God's will for your salvation. You've looked at it from the words spoken by Jesus and the actions of His disciples. The question of what **you must do** to be saved should be clear. You must **hear** God's Word, **believe** and **confess** Jesus is your lord and savior, **repent** by changing the way you think and act, and be **baptized** for the forgiveness of your sins.

LESSON 5

UNDERSTANDING GRACE

OBJECTIVE

The objective of this lesson is to understand God's greatest gift—grace.

KEY VERSE

"For by grace you have been saved through faith. And this is not your own doing; it is the gift of God, not a result of works, so that no one may boast."
Ephesians 2:8-9

KEY LESSON POINTS

Grace is at the center of God's plan of salvation.

Grace means undeserved favor.

Grace is the greatest news of all.

The word *grace* makes us think of wonderful hope and comfort. It is a word the apostle Paul loved to use. Every book of the Bible that he wrote (with the possible exception of Hebrews) begins and ends with the mention of this word. Grace is also talked about within his writings.

Grace is at the heart of God's plan of salvation. He granted grace the first time in man's history in the Garden of Eden when man sinned. Adam and Eve disobeyed God. But rather than destroying man and starting over, God made a way for man to come back to Him. He did not have to do that, but He did it because of His love for us. So that was the first time, but not the last time, God showed us grace.

The most common definition of God's grace is, "unmerited favor." This means that God blesses us in ways that we have not, do not, nor will ever deserve or be able to earn.

Someone else described grace as "blessings bestowed when wrath was owed." This goes a bit further in describing grace by showing that not only is the favor or blessings not deserved, but they have been given when what was deserved is God's punishment.

Another way to describe grace is with the letters G. R. A. C. E. Each letter stands for what grace is, "**G**od's **R**iches **A**t **C**hrist's **E**xpense." This means that the blessings we receive from God were given at the cost of Jesus' life.

ACTIVITY

Read the theme verse, Ephesians 2:8-9. Describe what you think is says in your own words. ____________________

____

____

____

Of the three ways to describe grace given in this lesson, which best explains it to you? And why? ____________________

____

____

____

Grace, Salvation, and Works

Grace is at the heart of our relationship with God. He gives it to us knowing that we cannot earn it, nor do we deserve it. Salvation through grace is a basic teaching of the Bible. In fact, Christianity is based on grace. There is no way we can become "Christ-like" if it were not for grace.

Man-made religions of the world are based on spending a life trying to be good enough or do enough to somehow try to earn God's favor. Part of the problem is that man-made or man-based religions are flawed in their beginning and flawed in their outcomes. They are flawed because God did not create them.

Grace does make demands of us. Grace demands an obedient faith. That means doing what we believe God wants us to do. In Acts 2 after Peter preached the first gospel sermon, the people hearing it cried out to him asking what they needed to do to escape God's punishment. Peter told them to show obedience by their repentance and baptism. In other words, they had to obey God's will. Since the New Testament had not been written yet, what Peter and the other apostles taught was what God wanted us to do.

But remember, as a wise man once said, "We do not work *for* our faith. We work *because* of our faith. Our faith, or belief and trust in God should cause us to want to do what God tells us to do. But the obedience does not earn salvation.

ACTIVITY

Read **Luke 17:7-10**. What did Jesus mean by His statement in verse 10? *"So you also, when you have done all that you were commanded, say, 'We are unworthy servants; we have only done what was our duty.'"*

____

____

____

____

____

____

A Great Example of Grace

Jesus taught many lessons to us by the use of parables. A parable is a story that teaches a lesson. One of the greatest parables is the parable of the Prodigal Son, found in Luke 15:11-32. In this great story, a man had two sons. The younger son wanted to leave and begin his own life, so he demanded his father give him the portion of inheritance due him. The father does so and soon afterward, the young man went away to a foreign land. While there, he wasted all the money he had. After it was all gone, everything turned bad. The land experienced bad times. His friends left him. The only job he could find was feeding pigs. He was so hungry and desperate that he even considered eating the pig's food. Then he remembered how good it was at his father's house. He remembered that even the servants were treated well. He decided he would return home. On the way he decided that he would ask his father to accept him, not as a son, but as a servant. As the son approached home, his father saw him and ran to greet him. The young son tried to tell his father how sorry he was and how he just wanted to be a servant. But the father wouldn't hear him. Instead he called for all to welcome the son home. He put new clothes on him along with a ring and shoes. He called for a party to honor his son's return. All of this was done to show that the father completely accepted the son back into the family.

Meanwhile, the older son, who had stayed home heard the noise. When he learned of his brother's return, he became angry and wouldn't even go in the house to join in the party. His father came out and pleaded for the son to come in but he still refused.

This great story is about how God welcomes home a sinner who has repented. It truly shows God's grace through the actions of the father. Some people would agree with the older son and demand justice for the younger son's wasteful life. Some might require mercy by saying that the father should demand the young son to work as a servant until he paid back what was wasted. But God offers grace by forgiving the sinner as the father in the story forgave the son completely, without reservation, and without making demands.

That is what God offers us when we realize our sin and turn to Him. He accepts us back and restores us into the family.

ACTIVITY

Read the following verses from the book of Hebrews, and state in your own words what you think the verse is saying.

Hebrews 12:15 ______________________________

____

____

____

Hebrews 12:28 ______________________________

____

____

____

Hebrews 13:9 ______________________________________

____

____

____

Hebrews 13:25 _____________________________________

____

____

____

Conclusion

When we understand what grace is, we praise God for His love for us. It causes us to want to do what God asks of us. He asks us first to return to Him. If for the first time, to become "in Christ" through baptism. If it is as the Prodigal Son did, it means to confess our sins, repent, and return to God. The promise in the story of the Prodigal Son is that God will welcome us back with open, loving arms.

Grace is the greatest news of all. Jesus completed the greatest act of grace by dying for us so that we can have our greatest need met, the need for forgiveness of sin and to be joined with God.

LESSON 6

DEALING WITH SIN

OBJECTIVE

To understand that we have a Savior who continues to cleanse us from sin.

KEY VERSE

"If we confess our sins, he is faithful and just to forgive us our sins and to cleanse us from all unrighteousness."

1 John 1:9

KEY LESSON POINTS

When we obey Jesus, we are freed from our sins.

Sin is breaking God's law.

If we confess our sins, God will forgive us.

When we obeyed Jesus through our confession, repentance, and baptism, we were freed from our sins. That's good news, but the news gets even better. God knows that we are not perfect and from time to time, even with the best of intentions, we still sin. So God in His marvelous plan not only made a way for us to be forgiven, but also a way for us to remain free from the consequences of sin. In this lesson, we will study what sin is and how to overcome the sin that continues to be a part of our lives.

What is sin?

The Bible describes sin as the breaking God's law (1 John 3:4). The meaning of sin is "to miss the mark" of what God says is goodness and holiness. Man has been missing the mark ever since the garden when Adam and Eve disobeyed God's simple command to not eat of the fruit from the tree of knowledge of good and evil (Genesis 2:16-17).

Who has sinned?

There are two simple verses in the Bible that clearly state that all of us have sinned. If we are honest, we will see that it is true.

ACTIVITY

How do you define sin?

____

____

____

Read Romans 3:26. State in your own words who has sinned.

____

____

____

Read 1 John 1:8. State in your own words what John says about someone who does not confess his or her sin.

___

___

___

The Really Good News!

You've already learned in an earlier lesson that you must believe that Jesus is your Lord and Savior, confess your sins, repent from your sinful life, and be baptized so that your sins will be forgiven (Acts 2:38). So we have Jesus whose death paid the price of our sins. In doing so, He established a way for us to come back to God and be free from the guilt and death as a result of our sin.

The question is, what happens after we are saved and sin again? John spoke about this in 1 John 2:1. Here's what he teaches us about the love that God has for those who have obeyed the gospel.

> *"My little children, I am writing these things to you so that you may not sin. But if anyone does sin, we have an advocate with the Father, Jesus Christ the righteous."*

This verse means that not only did Jesus die for our sins, but now, He is pleading our case before God. That's what an advocate is. An advocate is someone who speaks for us. It is one who presents us before the judge in a way to show why we should be forgiven. In this case, God is the judge and Jesus, God's son, is pleading our case for us.

ACTIVITY

Look again at what John says in 1 John 2:1. How is that good news?

___

___

What does it mean to you that even when we make mistakes and sin that God is willing to forgive us?

____

____

____

Even Paul Knew Sin

We know that the apostle Paul was a special man who wrote many of the books in the New Testament. It would seem that this giant of faith would have no problems with sin, yet even Paul struggled with sin. We do not know what kind, but we do know from his own words that he sinned.

Read Romans 7:14-19. Notice the statements Paul says about sin in his life.

- He does not understand his own actions.
- He does what he hates rather than what he knows and wants to do.
- He acknowledges that nothing good is within him.
- He desires to do what is right but does wrong instead.

Doesn't that sound like us from time to time? We know we should not do something but do it anyway. We know we should do something but don't do it anyway. We're just like children sometimes. Yet just as we continue to love our children when they fail, God continues to love us and wants us to remain in His family. That's the wonderful news!

But notice that Paul ends his confession with a joyful statement in Romans 7:25 by saying,

> *"Thanks be to God through Jesus Christ our Lord! So then, I myself serve the law of God with my mind."*

He then goes on in the next chapter continuing to rejoice that we have Jesus who sets us free from sin. We must learn that God recognizes that we are not perfect and will sin. This does not mean we do so deliberately, but there are times in our weakness that we give in to sin. Sometimes it is by what we do and other times by what we don't do that we know we should.

ACTIVITY

How to you describe the difference between deliberate sin and sin that we don't mean to do?

____

____

____

List some ways we might sin by not doing what we should do.

____

____

____

Conclusion

Knowing that God will forgive us when we sin and turn to Him in repentance does not mean that we can sin all we want because of God's willingness to forgive. If that is our attitude, then we are in danger of losing our salvation. That is the point of 1 John 3:9. John is saying that our attitude toward sin is that we try to avoid it all we can because we know that it displeases God. We are now children of God and should seek to obey God to the best of our ability. But, even when we try our hardest, we still sometimes sin. That is why it is such wonderful news to know that God is willing to welcome us back and forgive us.

Is there some sin in your life with which you struggle? Know that you are not alone in it. All of us sin and need God's forgiveness.

In a quiet time take a few minutes to write down the major source of sin in your life of which you are aware. Then quietly and sincerely pray to God that you know of this sin and want to be forgiven for it. You also should pray that God will give you strength to overcome that sin.

In doing this you express your faith in God. Remember the theme verse that God is faithful. That means He will keep His promise. The promise is that He will forgive us when we turn back to Him.

LESSON 7

FAITH AND HOPE

OBJECTIVE

To understand the importance of faith and hope.

KEY VERSE

"And without faith it is impossible to please him, for whoever would draw near to God must believe that he exists and that he rewards those who seek him.
Hebrews 11:6

KEY LESSON POINTS

Faith makes us pleasing to God.

Even a small amount of faith helps us grow.

Faith must be an active belief.

In the previous lesson, you learned that grace is at the center of our relationship with God. We also read in Ephesians 2:8,

"For by grace you have been saved through faith..."

So grace and faith work together as we understand salvation and what God wants from us.

ACTIVITY

Read Hebrews 11:1. Explain in your own words what this verse is saying. ______________________________

____

____

____

If you have different versions of the Bible, read this same verse to see if there are any differences. How does it help you understand better what faith is? ______________________________

____

____

____

Understanding Faith

If you looked up the word faith in a dictionary, you would probably find a definition that says, "Unquestioning belief, complete trust or confidence." We use the word faith to describe our beliefs, actions, and our conduct in our relationship with God. We often think of faith as something of which we have a large amount to do great things for our Lord or to become who our Lord wants us to be. This is not necessarily true. We will see later that even a small, but growing faith is powerful.

Something Jesus said many times was, "Oh you of little faith."

One time Jesus used this expression and explained how much faith was needed to do what God wants. In Matthew 17:20 we read,

> *"He said to them, 'Because of your little faith. For truly, I say to you, if you have faith like a grain of mustard seed, you will say to his mountain, "Move from here to there,' and it will move, and nothing will be impossible for you."*

When Jesus said this, He had just been through what was called the Transfiguration during which the apostles saw Him talking with Moses and the prophet Elijah, and heard God's voice telling them to listen to Jesus. Jesus had also healed a boy who was overcome by demons. Jesus used these events to show them how they, too, would be able to do great things for the Lord if they developed faith. But in His teachings, He said that only the amount of a mustard seed, among the smallest of seeds, and not some great depth of faith would be enough for them to do great things.

Although you want your faith to be as strong as it can be, don't miss an important point here. If you want to please God and do great things for Him, even a small but believing and trusting faith will allow you to begin to do so. Growing in your faith helps you be an even more faithful servant to God.

ACTIVITY

Why do you think God does not require us to have a great or complete faith in order to please Him?

____

____

____

Do you agree or disagree with the following statement, and why? "If we only need a little bit of faith to please God and do wonderful things for him, then we don't have to develop a strong faith."

Faith and Belief

Faith is more than just believing something. Faith is an active belief. Read James 1:3. It tells us that faith produces steadfastness and steadfastness, when mature, leads us to be complete.

James isn't talking about having everything we need in our lives to make us rich and comfortable, but to provide us with all we need to serve God.

In James 2:14 James tells us that faith is an active process. He did not say we work to earn our faith. Our work *shows* our faith. He gives an example of work in the following verses where he explains about doing something good for someone, not just talking about it.

ACTIVITY

What does *steadfastness* mean?

What does *mature* mean?

Read James 2:18-19. What is James saying here about faith and works?

Read James 2:26. What is James saying here about faith and works?

____

____

God's Strength, Not Ours

Earlier the question was asked why God only requires a small amount of faith for us to be pleasing to Him. One answer is that through our weaknesses God is glorified because we recognize we cannot do anything except by God's power, not ours. As our faith grows we learn to trust more and more in our Lord and not in ourselves. If God is working through us, then we become stronger and more able to do His will.

Understanding Hope

Hope is another word we read in Hebrews 11:1. A common misunderstanding about hope is that it is a vague wish for something to happen, a strong desire. For example someone might say, "I hope it rains." Or another say, "I hope it doesn't rain." But hope that the Bible describes is not vague wishing or even strong desire but rather a ***confident assurance*** based on how God has always kept His promises. So when God says that He promises salvation to those that have obeyed Him, then we know He will do so. In other words, you can and do have hope!

ACTIVITY

Read Hebrews 11:1. Notice three key words in this Scripture: *faith, assurance,* and *hope.* To what do these lead?

____

____

____

What is the difference between a vague feeling that you want something to happen and confidence that it will happen?

____

____

____

Conclusion

Faith is critical for us to grow into who God wants us to be – like Christ. Without it, we are not even able to begin growing. Faith is not some power of positive thinking but rather believing and trusting in God and doing what God wills for us.

Faith is a critical part of our relationship with God. God's grace saves us, but it is through obedient faith that we receive his grace. This means we not only believe, but act as God wants us to in that belief.

And because our faith grows, we also see our hope, or confident assurance, growing.

LESSON 8

MAKING THE ANGELS REJOICE

OBJECTIVE

The objective of this lesson is to understand the importance of repentance.

KEY VERSE

"Just so, I tell you, there is joy before the angels of God over one sinner who repents."

Luke 15:10

KEY LESSON POINTS

Repentance means turning away from sin.

Repentance means to stop rejecting Jesus.

Repentance makes the angels rejoice.

Understanding Repentance

Usually when someone mentions the word *repent* we think of "turning from sin." That is part of the meaning of repentance, but there is more than that. When we see it in the Bible, it is associated with changing our way of thinking and turning from sin. So a better understanding of repentance as God's Word teaches us is a change of mind that results in a change of how we act.

ACTIVITY

Read the passages below from your Bible, and write in your own words what each is saying.

Acts 2:38 ______________________________

____

____

____

Acts 3:19 ______________________________

____

____

____

Acts 17:30 ______________________________

____

____

____

Acts 26:20 ______________________________

____

____

____

In each of the references above, what is the key word related to repentance or is a result of our repentance?

____

____

____

Repentance and Your Salvation

To repent in relation to your salvation is to change how you think about Jesus. Repentance and faith are seen as two parts of the same idea. It is impossible to place your faith in Jesus as your Savior without first changing your mind about who He is and what He has done. Whether from your rejection of Him or from not knowing about Him, it is a change of your mind. So biblical repentance, in relation to salvation, is to change your mind from rejecting Jesus or not knowing Jesus to accepting and placing your faith in Him.

As with all other issues related to salvation, please understand that your action of repentance is not something you do to "earn" salvation. It is how you follow-through with your understanding and acceptance of Jesus. It is always by the grace of God that we are saved (Ephesians 2:8). Repenting also is not a one-time event, but involves continually turning from sin. Satan tries to destroy our faith by tempting us to sin. We must constantly be on guard to resist temptations to sin. James 1:4 tells us,

> *"Submit yourselves therefore to God. Resist the devil, and he will flee from you."*

Making the Angels Rejoice

The theme verse for this lesson, Luke 15:10, is from one of three powerful lessons Jesus taught. In the context of these lessons, some of the religious leaders of Jesus' time were complaining that Jesus was associating with people that they considered to be of the worst sort. Jesus decided to teach them about how much God loves everyone, especially someone who realizes their sin and wants to turn back to Him (repentance). Each of the three lessons He taught were on the same subject.

The first lesson was about a shepherd who had 100 sheep, but one had wandered off. So the shepherd made sure the 99 remaining were taken care of and went off in search of the one that was lost. When he found it, he rejoiced with his neighbors and friends.

In the second lesson Jesus teaches about a woman who had lost one of 10 coins, so she lit a candle and cleaned her entire house looking for it. Then when she found it, she called together her friends and neighbors and shared the joy with them. Again, Jesus is teaching that everyone is important, even one soul that is lost. And when that lost person is restored to God, there is great rejoicing in heaven. The image of the angels rejoicing before God means that not only is God pleased, but all the beings of heaven rejoice as well.

Then Jesus taught a third lesson called the Prodigal Son. We've covered this story in an earlier lesson. Notice that there was great rejoicing over the younger son's return. But the older son was not rejoicing. In fact, he was quite angry that the father was treating the younger son so well and had never treated him to any kind of party even though he had remained faithful all this time.

In this third lesson Jesus was clearly teaching the religious leaders that they should not be angry when Jesus associated with the ones they looked down on. In fact, they should also have been associating with them and to rejoice and welcome them back when they turned from their sinful life.

That is the lesson for us today. We must first make certain that we repent and then help others to turn to God and gain the same salvation we enjoy. And we should be overjoyed when they do.

ACTIVITY

Read again the theme verse for this lesson from Luke 15:10. Why would the angels rejoice over one sinner who repents?

____

____

____

Looking at all three of the lessons Jesus taught in Luke 15, what is the reaction of the one who found what was lost and what should be our reaction as well?

____

____

____

Conclusion

Repenting is one of the most powerful things we can do. It is both a changing of our minds and a changing of how we live. The changing of our minds is about how we think and our attitudes about the world around us. We change from focus on self to focus on what pleases God. We do it because we recognize that God loves us so much that He gave Jesus as a sacrifice for our sins. And in our response to that love, we seek to honor God by the way we think and behave.

LESSON 9

DISCOVERING GOD'S WILL

OBJECTIVE

The objective of this lesson is for us to understand how to discover God's will for our lives.

KEY VERSE

"Therefore do not be foolish, but understand what the will of the Lord is."

Ephesians 5:17

KEY LESSON POINTS

God wants us to know and do His will.

We are servants to the Master.

God gives us His will through the Bible.

If you are a child of God, then you should want to do God's will more than anything else. A question asked many times is, "What is God's will?" or "How do I know I am doing God's will?" These are good questions and ones that we should always be asking. Sometimes we feel it is hard to know God's will for a certain situation, but in reality, it is not. Always remember that God wants us to know His will, so He clearly reveals it to us through His written Word.

Those in the kingdom of God are often described as servants, a description Jesus used to not only describe Himself, but His followers as well. He stated that the greatest in the kingdom was the one who served (Matthew 18:1-5). One general characteristic of a servant is that he or she seeks to do what the master desires. It is all the more important that we, as servants of God, seek to discover and carry out God's will in our lives and in ways that positively impact the lives of others.

Many people misunderstand the idea of discovering and doing God's will. They want God's will to be something they already are doing or want to do. For example, sometimes we might have our minds made up about something and then try to prove either through our reasoning or by some verse in Scripture that what we wanted to do all along is God's will. This is dangerous since what we want may in fact be contrary to God's will. Remember, we are the servant. God is the master. Our role is to do His will.

Another mistake is to think that God has an exact plan for every aspect of our lives, so we want to learn exactly what it is that God wants us to do in a situation. This is also not correct. God granted us a wonderful gift, the ability to choose. This is known as "free will." This means that sometimes God leaves the decisions up to us. He clearly gives us principles (general guidelines) in His Word and sometimes direct commands to do something or to not do something. But many times He leaves the choices up to us. For example, God does not tell us to marry a specific person. He wants us to marry someone who will support and encourage us and seek to strengthen our relationship with God. God does not tell us to prepare for a specific career, but He did give us knowledge and abilities, what we call talents, so that we can be successful in a chosen career. He does tell us in His Word that whatever we do, we should do it as if we are doing it for Him. In other words, we glorify God with everything about our lives (Colossians 3:17 and Colossians 3:23).

ACTIVITY

Read the following verses. Some tell clearly what God's will is. Some provide general guidelines. After reading the verse, write what you see as God's will in it.

Romans 12:2 ______________________________

____

____

____

1 Thessalonians 4:3-5 ______________________________

____

____

____

1 John 2:16-17 ______________________________

____

____

____

Matthew 7:21-23 ______________________________

____

____

____

1 Peter 2:15 ______________________________

____

____

____

Ephesians 5:15-20 __________________________

____

____

____

1 Timothy 2:4 ______________________________

____

____

____

Doing God's Will

It is just as important not only to know God's will but to do what God wants us to do. In Matthew 21:28-32 Jesus told a story about a father with two sons. The father told his sons to go work in the vineyard. The first son refused to do so but later obeyed and went to work. The second son said he would but later disobeyed and refused to go to work. Jesus then asked which of the two sons actually did the will of the father. The obvious answer is the first son who actually went to work in the orchard. To those who were listening to the story, Jesus was telling them that the will of God is that we repent of our sins and obey God. To us it means that we repent of our sins and obey the gospel. When we do that we are turning away from *"My Will"* and turning toward, *"Thy Will."* If we have not done that, then anything else we do or don't do is not important.

Sometimes God reveals His will to us clearly and other times it seems to take a while to know what His will is. We could compare this to turning on a light in the middle of the night. We've all experienced being initially blinded by the light when we turn the light on in a dark room. This shows how sometimes God knows we need to see things gradually and reveals it to us as we are prepared to receive it.

Another example is when a child wants to do something but doesn't because his parent has communicated not to do whatever it is. The child wants to please the parent, so he doesn't do it. If he disobeys and does it, then it is clearly wrong. That is what sin is: disobeying God's will. Has a child ever told you something like, "Well, you didn't tell me to not do that." We know that the child has the reasoning ability to know that if we told him not to do something in one situation then it is probably true that we don't want him to do it in a similar situation. That is how God sometimes reveals His will to us. He doesn't have to tell us every single *do* or *don't*. He has given us the ability to understand from His Word that if something is against His will in one situation, then it is also against His will in another similar situation. In situations where He doesn't give us a specific command not to do something or to do something, then He gives us guiding principles.

ACTIVITY

Read Matthew 7:24-27. What is the point Jesus is making about doing His will?

____

____

____

Why would God give us both general guidelines and specific commands?

Read Matthew 7:21-23. What is the point Jesus is making?

Read Psalm 37:4. Write what you feel this verse is saying.

Conclusion

It is important to discover God's will whether you are a Christian or someone who has not yet obeyed our Lord. To the one already a Christian, it is important because we are now servants of the Master and seek to do what He wants us to do. We do so because we recognize that God loves us, and we seek to honor and glorify Him with our lives.

If someone has not obeyed the Lord to become a Christian, then the most important thing is to learn that what God wants is for that person to obey the gospel and become a child of God.

God wants us to know and obey His will. That is why we find His will all throughout His Word in the Bible. If we are earnestly seeking, God will make it clear to us. The key is wanting God's will, not our own.

LESSON 10

BEARING FRUIT

OBJECTIVE

The objective of this lesson is to understand the importance of bearing fruit as a Christian.

KEY VERSE

"By this my Father is glorified, that you bear much fruit... "

John 15:8

KEY LESSON POINTS

A faithful Christian must bear fruit.

Showing Jesus to others is one way to bear fruit.

Growing spiritually is one way to bear fruit.

In an earlier lesson, you learned that being a Christian is being a servant of God. You also learned that the main thing we are to do, no matter what we do, is to glorify God. One of the most important ways we glorify God is by helping others learn about God so they also have the chance to become Christians. This is what we mean by bearing fruit.

Bearing fruit is a way of saying that we add value or bring reward to something. In the case of our relationship with God, it means that we add value to what Jesus did for us by dying on the cross. It means that His death means something.

Two Types of Fruit

The type of fruit we produce as a Christian can be divided into two types: internal fruit and external fruit. Internal fruit is the change we experience as we grow as a Christian and become who God wants us to be. This is also known as "fruit of the Spirit." Galatians 5:22-23 lists the fruit of the Spirit. Notice that all of these are internal to the life of a Christian although they are shown by the life we lead. Also notice that Paul says that there is no law against these. This means that not only are they right, but there is also no limit to them. The more we grow spiritually, the more these should be seen in our lives. It is one way we see that we are growing spiritually.

ACTIVITY

Read Galatians 5:22-23. List the nine fruit of the Spirit.

1. ______________________
2. ______________________
3. ______________________
4. ______________________
5. ______________________
6. ______________________
7. ______________________
8. ______________________
9. ______________________

We also said there is external fruit that we produce. This means that we take the fruit of the Spirit we are developing and show Jesus to those around us. We teach Jesus to the world so that everyone has a chance to become a child of God. That is what it means to produce external fruit.

In Matthew 13, Jesus tells a wonderful story about a farmer who went out to plant some seeds. He scattered the seeds over his field. Not all the seeds landed in good soil so that they would grow. Some seeds fell on the pathway and never grew because the birds came by and ate them. Other seeds fell on rocky soil where they grew but were not able to keep growing and the sun came out and dried them up. Some seed fell among some thorns that choked out the plants. Finally, some seed fell on good soil and grew to produce a large crop.

ACTIVITY

Read Matthew 13:18-23. What did Jesus say for each of the types of soil on which the seeds landed?

The pathway – ______________________________

____

____

The rocky soil – ____________________________

____

____

The thorns – _______________________________

____

____

The good soil – ______________________________

____

____

Not Bearing Fruit

A sign of a healthy plant is that it bears fruit. If it does not, then the farmer will take time to try to make the plant healthy. If that doesn't work, then the farmer will cut down or remove the plant and toss it away.

Jesus teaches us a lesson about this in John 15. First, He tells us that if we stay connected to Him, then we will bear much fruit. But He also tells us that if we are away from Him, then we will not bear fruit. He says that the branch that is not connected will be removed and destroyed. The clear lesson here is that we must remain faithful to Him so that we will bear fruit that glorifies Him and helps us bear fruit as He asks.

What should you do if you think you aren't bearing fruit? There are times when you may not be doing what God wants you to do to bear fruit. When you think this is happening, you have to look at yourself and question what is going on in your life. The answer might be that you aren't spending enough time in prayer and studying God's Word. It might be that you aren't looking for opportunities to show Jesus to others. It might be that you have let the things in your life or that are around you interfere with your devotion to God. Whatever the reason, you must identify it and remove it.

It might be that you don't see the issue yourself. Here are some things you can do specifically to help.

- Discuss it with a friend or someone you trust.
- Pray about the situation or issue.
- Look harder for opportunities to love and serve.
- Begin serving in a new area of work.
- Get more involved in personal as well as public Bible study.

Conclusion

Remember, we are the servants, and God is the master. As servants who want to do as the master says, we grow spiritually, and we show Jesus to others.

Each of us has different levels of abilities. The great thing is that God asks us to do the best we can with the abilities we have. All of us can do something to show Jesus to others. In the list of the fruit of the Spirit, each one of us can develop these in our lives. And when we do, we will be able to show Jesus to others in our own way.

LESSON 11

SPIRITUAL GROWTH

OBJECTIVE

The objective of this lesson is to learn how to mature spiritually.

KEY VERSE

"Therefore let us leave the elementary doctrine of Christ and go on to maturity, not laying again a foundation of repentance from dead works and of faith toward God,"

Hebrews 6:1

KEY LESSON POINTS

Spiritual growth is a journey to become like Christ.

Spiritual growth means doing what God wills.

We must grow to become like Jesus.

In life we understand the importance of maturity. Growing and maturing brings challenges and concerns, but it also brings rewards. The same is true of spiritual maturity. Maturing in Christ has challenges and concerns, but the rewards, as God promises, are wonderful beyond our understanding. One reward is a greater knowledge of how God works in our lives. Another is a stronger faith, which makes us pleasing to God (Hebrews 11:6).

Spiritual growth is not a destination. It is a journey we travel through all our lives as children of God.

We know that if we are not growing physically, then we are not healthy. It is also true that if we are not growing intellectually and emotionally, then we are at a disadvantage in life. It is also true that we must grow spiritually. But unlike the other areas of growth, there is no limit to our spiritual growth.

ACTIVITY

These questions don't require you to write anything down, but you should think about how you would respond.

If you looked at your regular day, how much time do you spend in each of the following?

- Physical development
- Intellectual/Emotional development
- Spiritual development

Given where you are in your life in terms of age, job, family, marriage, or any other areas, do you feel comfortable with how you spend time in each category? If not, then how can you improve?

What is Spiritual Growth?

Spiritual growth means to keep growing until we become who God wants us to be. God wants us to be as much like Jesus as we can. That is what it means to be a Christian, to be "Christ-like." No matter who you are or how long you've been in God's family, there is still room to grow and mature. Another way to explain spiritual growth is putting into practice what we learn from God's Word. It is a lifelong process.

ACTIVITY

Read the following Bible verses, and state in your own words what they say about spiritual growth.

1 Peter 2:1-2 ______________________________

____

____

____

2 Peter 1:5-8 ______________________________

____

____

____

2 Peter 3:18 ______________________________

____

____

____

Hebrews 5:11-14 ____________________________

____

____

____

Hebrews 6:1-2 ____

____

____

____

Conclusion

Our spiritual journey begins the moment we respond to the gospel. From that point on our responsibility is to grow in Christlikeness. Spiritual growth requires focus in three areas:

- Growing in our understanding of what it means to be a Christian.
- Expanding our personal knowledge of God's Word.
- Applying what we learn from God's Word to our lives every day.

LESSON 12

WORSHIP IN SPIRIT AND IN TRUTH

OBJECTIVE

The objective for this lesson is to understand how we draw closer to God through our worship.

KEY VERSE

"God is spirit, and those who worship him must worship in spirit and truth."
John 4:24

KEY LESSON POINTS

We worship God and encourage each other.

Worship means we praise God.

True worship is God-centered.

One of the blessings as well as an important responsibility for the Christian is the practice of coming together with other Christians to worship God. There is a purpose for this beyond simply obeying the command of God to honor Him. Our worship the first day of the week is perhaps our most common and visible way in which we can draw closer to God. It should be a natural and desired activity. Worship, however, should not be restricted to just that time. We come together on the first day of the week, as God commands. At this time, we hear God's Word, pray, sing, take the Lord's supper, and make an offering. These are only the more visible elements of worship. Remember, our objective is to grow closer to God.

What is worship?

Worship of God means we praise God as we speak, sing, and express otherwise how good and powerful God is. We worship either in formal or informal ways.

Formal worship is coming together in an organized worship service. We are commanded, or at the very least, strongly encouraged to worship. Not only are we commended, but we also see by example from the Bible that worship was something God's people desired to do regularly and often.

Informal worship is the life we live each day that is focused on honoring and obeying God. It is our personal study of God's Word and time spent in prayer and thinking about God. It is also the time we show acts of love and kindness. It is how we live our lives focused and dedicated to God.

ACTIVITY

Read Hebrews 10:25. What does it say about worship?

____

____

____

Read Acts 2:24-47. What does this say about the early Christians and their desire to worship?

Worshiping in spirit and truth

True worship is God-centered worship. Some tend to get caught up in place, actions, and appearances. Although these have importance, they are not what God wants from us first. He first wants a true and open heart (Psalm 51:16; Isaiah 1:11). God-centered worship also means that it is reserved for God. True worship honors God with love and submission that includes acts of adoration (i.e. songs of praise, prayers honoring God).

Concerning the "spirit" aspect of worship, we can do all the things we do in worship, but if our heart is not focused on God, then we are nothing more than what Paul compared to our actions without love – a "noisy gong or a clanging cymbal" (1 Corinthians 13:1). In other words, that "worship" has no value.

ACTIVITY

Read Romans 12:1-2. What does Paul mean by offering ourselves as a living sacrifice and our spiritual worship?

Drawing closer to God through our worship

We can draw closer to God during worship by being aware of those among us. First we worship with our fellow members as the family of God. We also worship with our visitors who see the love we have for our Lord and each other as well as the joy we have in worshiping and serving our Lord. But most importantly, we understand that God is with us when we worship. Remembering all of this keeps us focused on Him.

ACTIVITY

Sometimes people feel they have not gotten anything from the time spent worshiping. What are some ways to get the most from our time spent with God in worship?

____

____

____

____

____

____

Conclusion

Worship is more than a command, it is a privilege. We should develop the attitude of, "I get to" not, "I have to."

We should have the same outlook David expressed in Psalm 122:1,

> *"I was glad when they said to me, 'Let us go into the house of the LORD.'"*

One of the greatest spiritual blessings we enjoy as Christians in this life is the fellowship we share in our public assemblies. What an honor it is that God opens up to us so that we can draw closer to Him!

LESSON 13

JUDGMENT DAY

OBJECTIVE

The objective of this lesson is to understand judgment day.

KEY VERSE

"And just as it is appointed for man to die once, and after that comes judgment,"

Hebrews 9:27

KEY LESSON POINTS

Judgment means to give account to God for our lives.

Only God knows when judgment will happen.

We must be ready for God to return.

Judgment is something each of us will face one day. To the one who has obeyed our Lord in salvation and has lived a faithful life, this is not a day to fear, but a day to rejoice. It is a day when God rewards those who remained faithful servants. The overwhelming majority of those faithful servants have gone through their lives unknown to others but not on judgment day. On that day, those previously known only by God will become known to all. On that day, those servants will hear, "Well done, good and faithful servant." Sadly, for those who have rejected God and embraced the world, it will be the most horrible day in their existence.

Also judgment is not the day in which our salvation will be determined. That has already been determined when we obeyed the gospel.

What is Judgment?

Judgment is when we give an account of our lives in service to God (Romans 14:12). This is described by Jesus in what we call the Parable of the Talents (Matthew 25:14-30).

In this parable, Jesus teaches that a man went on a journey and gave three of his servants an amount of money called *talents*. To one he gave five talents, another two, and another one. The man with five talents used it to make five more. The man with two talents used it to make two more. The man with one talent didn't do anything with it. When the man returned, each servant presented what had been done with the talents in his care. The servants with five and two talents were rewarded, but the one with one talent was punished because he did not use what the master had given him.

This parable tells us what judgment will be like. If we have not done as God expects of us, then we will be punished for not having faithfully served our master.

ACTIVITY

Read Acts 17:31.

What is Paul saying in the passage?

Who is the "man of righteousness" of whom Paul speaks?

What Will Happen at Judgment?

First, the judge will be Jesus. This is stated by Jesus Himself in John 5:22-27.

> *"The Father judges no one, but has given all judgment to the Son, that all may honor the Son, just as they honor the Father"* (22-23).

The standard against which we are judged is the teachings of Jesus (John 12:48). That is why we must learn, understand, and obey what Jesus teaches us as found in the Bible.

In Matthew 22:36-40 we see some more information about this. One day a young man asked Jesus what was the greatest commandment. Jesus answered that we must love God with all our heart, soul, and mind. He also said that we must love our neighbor as ourselves. So if we obey the teachings of Jesus, we will demonstrate our love for God and our love for our fellow man.

Next we can find in the Bible who will be judged. The angels that sinned against God and were cast out of heaven will be judged (2 Peter 2:4). Also all mankind, from all of history and those living at the time of the return of Jesus will be judged (1 Peter 4:17).

At judgment, we will answer for what we have done, spoken, and thought in this life (1 Timothy 5:24-25). This is an important reason why we must do everything we can to live a life that God wants us to do.

When Will Judgment Happen?

First of all, the right question to ask is, "Will we be ready for judgment?" This means we must be in Christ and living faithfully.

In Matthew 24 we read some important teachings by Jesus about the end of the age, or judgment day. One day Jesus made a comment to His disciples about the destruction of the temple in Jerusalem. He had stated that the temple would be completely destroyed. This greatly bothered the disciples so later they asked Him a direct question about it. Jesus answered with two responses. The first was directly focused on the destruction of the temple. He gave details about what would be going on at the time and so they would be ready. But remember, this was in direct response to the question about the destruction of the temple.

But the question asked by the disciples was a two-part question. The second part of the question was about signs of the returning of Jesus and the end of the age. To this question Jesus provides some additional figurative language but gives the key to the answer in verse 36. He stated,

> *"But concerning that day and hour no one knows, not even the angels of heaven, nor the Son, but the Father only."*

He gives one more important response in verse 44. Here he states what is the really important point,

> *"Therefore you also must be ready, for the Son of Man is coming at an hour you do not expect."*

Jesus then goes on to tell a series of parables and teachings about being prepared. These teachings cover all of Matthew 24 and 25. The ones who should fear judgment are those who do not heed what Jesus teaches in these chapters and are not prepared.

ACTIVITY

Who will be our judge? ______________________________

What is the standard by which we will be judged?

____

Who will be judged? ________________________________

On what will we be judged? __________________________

____

When will Judgment Day happen? ____________________

What is the most important point that Jesus teaches in Matthew 24 and 25? ________________________________

____

____

Conclusion

It is normal that we would be concerned, even afraid of the concept of judgment. But God's Word teaches in several places that we should not fear judgment but actually look forward to it. One of the most important teachings is found in 1 John 1:7-9.

> *"But if we walk in the light, as he is in the light, we have fellowship with one another, and the blood of Jesus his Son cleanses us from all sin. If we say we have no sin, we deceive ourselves, and the truth is not in us. If we confess our sins,*

*he is faithful and just to forgive us our sins and to cleanse us from all unrighteous*ness."

To those who have obeyed God's Word, there is hope for eternal life because we know we have been forgiven for our sins. This is the teaching from Romans 5:10-11.

"For if while we were enemies we were reconciled to God by the death of his Son, much more, now that we are reconciled, shall we be saved by his life. More than that, we also rejoice in God through our Lord Jesus Christ, through whom we have now received reconciliation."

NOTES

www.ingramcontent.com/pod-product-compliance
Lightning Source LLC
LaVergne TN
LVHW020646100826
845148LV00012B/2348

9780890988886